Ideal Voice and Speech Training

A Book of Exercises

Ken Parkin

A SAMUEL FRENCH ACTING EDITION

SAMUEL
FRENCH

FOUNDED 1830

SAMUELFRENCH-LONDON.CO.UK
SAMUELFRENCH.COM

FOREWORD

It gives me great satisfaction to know that Speech training is becoming an important factor in education. Many schools now employ a full-time specialist in the subject and indications suggest that these posts will become even more frequent in the future.

In the preface to *Pygmalion*, George Bernard Shaw remarks that "The English have no respect for their language, and will not teach their children to speak it". This may have been true of the 1920's when the play was published, but Technical Colleges such as the one of which I am Principal are proving the antithesis of this remark.

Mr Parkin's lessons have aimed at (*a*) a greater self-confidence, (*b*) clear and unaffected speech, (*c*) a wider understanding and appreciation of the Spoken Word; and the results of his work have always been apparent and most successful. He is a remarkable teacher, with a tremendous belief in all that he teaches. Thousands of students owe him a great debt of gratitude, for the confidence which he has created in them.

May this little book have the success which it undoubtedly deserves.

J. H. ANDERSON, BSc(Eng)
AMIMarE, FRSA

INTRODUCTION

This small book contains sets of exercises which have been compiled for their practical value in the art of Speech training. Every exercise included has been used in the classes which I have conducted and I have every faith in their effectiveness.

Today, more than ever before, a clear and attractive speaking voice is vital to the student if he wishes to gain promotion in a highly competitive world, and Oral English is gaining importance in our Universities and Training Colleges. It is of immense psychological value to the individual to be able to express himself with ease and to be able to communicate without a feeling of inferiority. In fact, to face the world with grace and self-confidence.

KEN PARKIN
1962

HAMLET'S ADVICE TO THE PLAYERS

Speak the speech, I pray you, as I pronounced it to you, trippingly on the tongue: but if you mouth it, as many of your players do, I had as lief the town-crier spoke my lines. Nor do not saw the air too much with your hand, thus, but use all gently; for in the very torrent, tempest, and, as I may say, the whirlwind of passion, you must acquire and beget a temperance that may give it smoothness. O, it offends me to the soul to hear a robustious periwig-pated fellow tear a passion to tatters, to very rags, to split the ears of the groundlings, who for the most part are capable of nothing but inexplicable dumb-shows and noise: I would have such a fellow whipped for o'erdoing Termagant; it out-herods Herod: pray you, avoid it.

Be not too tame neither, but let your own discretion be your tutor: suit the action to the word, the word to the action; with this special observance, that you o'erstep not the modesty of nature: for anything so overdone is from the purpose of playing, whose end, both at the first and now, was and is, to hold, as 'twere, the mirror up to nature; to show virtue her own feature, scorn her own image, and the very age and body of the time his form and pressure. Now this overdone, or come tardy off, though it make the unskilful laugh, cannot but make the judicious grieve; the censure of the which one must in your allowance o'erweigh a whole theatre of others. O, there be players that I have seen play, and heard others praise, and that highly, not to speak it profanely, that, neither having the accent of Christians nor the gait of Christian, pagan, nor man, have so strutted and bellowed that I have thought some of nature's journeymen had made men and not made them well, they imitated humanity so abominably . . . O, reform it altogether. And let those that play your clowns speak no more than is set down for them; for there be of them that will themselves laugh, to set on some quantity of barren specta-tors to laugh too; though, in the meantime, some necessary question of the play be then to be considered: that's villanous, and shows a most pitiful ambition in the fool that uses it. Go, make you ready.
Hamlet, iii, 2.

RELAXATION

Tension in any part of the body immediately has a constricting influence on the human voice and so it is important that the student begins each practice session with the following exercise in relaxation.

(a) Stand up. Stretch the body from head to toe making every muscle stiff and tense.

(b) Slowly relax each part of the body in turn, beginning with the head and face muscles, the jaw and the tongue, the neck and the shoulders, the chest and the spine, around the waist, down to the knees and to the ankles. Finally relax the arms down to the wrists and to the finger-tips.

(c) Drop forward from the waist allowing the head and arms to hang heavily.

(d) Slowly unwind the spine, bringing the head up last so that the body is in a *relaxed easily held stance*.

The importance of complete relaxation cannot be overstressed because it is only when the body is relaxed that the mind can be fully creative.

Posture

Practice standing well. Keep the weight evenly balanced over the balls of your feet. Shoulders well down, hands relaxed by your sides. Try standing against a wall and feel your head, shoulders, buttocks and calves touching it. In other words STAND TALL.

Always sit with your trunk straight and not bent forward, backward, or to one side. Allow the chair to support you. That is what a chair is for.

I

Walk with your feet pointed forward and your legs swinging from the hips. Take regular steps. Hold the abdomen well in. Head high and chin well in. Smile to avoid any tenseness of the facial and neck muscles which are the cause of much fatigue. *Bend from the knees* if you have to pick something from the ground.

Breathing and Breath Control

Breath is the motive power of Speech and so it is well to devote much of your early practice to the correct application of breathing exercises.

Exercise One

(a) Standing relaxed. Place your hands against your lower ribs (at the sides of the rib cage) and breathe in to a mental count of three. Do not allow your shoulders to rise.

(b) Breathe out to a mental count of three (feeling for rib swing).

Exercise Two

(a) Breathe in to a count of three.

(b) Hold the breath without breathing in or out for a count of three.

(c) Breathe out to a count of three.

(It is a good plan to leave the jaw open during this exercise to prove that the breath is being held on the diaphragm and not in the throat)

Exercise Three

Breathe in for a count of five, whilst swinging the arms sideways shoulder high. Turn the palms over whilst holding the breath for a count of five, then let them swing slowly downwards for a count of ten, whilst breathing out.

Exercise Four

Breathe in to a count of three.
Hold breath for a count of three.
Expel breath whilst humming M, evenly and slowly, for a count of ten, keeping the ribs extended and expelling the air by means of pulling in the upper abdominal muscles, which control the diaphragm. To do this, rest the back of the left hand against the side ribs and the palm of the right hand on the upper part of the abdomen, above the waist and immediately below the ribs.

(This exercise is also good for resonance. As are 8, 9 and 10)

Exercise Five

As for Exercise Four only no·v expel breath on a steady hiss-S.

Exercise Six

As for Exercise Four only expel breath whilst counting aloud to 10, then 15, then 20.

Exercise Seven

As for Exercise Four only expel breath whilst repeating the complete alphabet, the days of the week, or the months of the year.

Exercise Eight

To develop the strength and flexibility of the diaphragm, take in a full breath then pant (like a dog) feeling for the movement of the diaphragm in the midriff region.

Exercise Nine

Hum an M sound for about three seconds, then drop jaw for an AH sound and sustain this until the breath is almost expended and then close the lips again so that the exercise finishes on the M sound once more. (There should be no break between the M and AH sounds.)

Exercise Ten

Repeat the foregoing exercise with the OO, OH, and EE sounds framed by the M.

M——AH——M	M——OO——M
M——OH——M	M——EE——M

The lips should tickle and buzz on M.

Exercise Eleven

Repeat BIMMA BOOMA, BIMMA BOOMA, sending the sound into the mask of the face. Also try, Ding Dong, Ding Dong, all the bells are ringing.

Exercise Twelve

Glide up and down the scale, keeping the sound forward all the time, whilst

(a) Humming the M sound.

(b) Forming the AH sound. Then repeat the exercise with the OO, OH and EE sounds separately.

(c) Gliding from one vowel sound to the next. E.g. AH—OH—OO—EE.

Breath control comes easily to some people whilst others need to work at it for some time before it becomes second nature.

ARTICULATION

Clear articulation is always the result of a flexible jaw, lips and tongue. The following exercises on these individual organs plus the tongue twisters and the work on the vowel and consonant charts should establish firmly a crispness of utterance. (*See Consonant Chart on page 27*)

Jaw Exercises

Yawn with the mouth well open.

Stroke the jaw with the index fingers all down the jawbone until the mouth falls easily open.

Repeat—L.L. Lah—L.L. Lah—L.L. Lah—Lah. Dropping the jaw on the ah each time. *Do this exercise with all the consonants in turn.*

Wedge Exercise

Cut a triangular piece of cardboard about two inches wide. Hold it vertically between the finger and thumb, and with a rhythmic wrist movement place the apex between the teeth for the AH sounds and away from the mouth for the SHE. The finger and thumb can be used instead of a wedge.

SA	KA	SHE	FA	RA
KA	KA	SHE	FA	RA
RA	KA	SHE	FA	RA
DA	KA	SHE	FA	RA
FA	KA	SHE	FA	RA

Exercise for the Lips

Pout the lips forward and then stretch them sideways. (Broad OO and EE sound)

Repeat vowels. (OO. AH.-OO. AH) and (OO. OH. AW. AH. AY. EE)

Curl your upper lip and try to touch your nose with it.

Curl your lower lip and try to touch your chin with it.

Exercise for the Tongue

Point the tongue out and then point it from side to side, and then up and down.

Place tongue tip against the lower teeth and then push out the centre.

Move the tip of the tongue from behind the top teeth to behind the lower teeth, up and down, about a dozen times. The jaw should be kept open whilst this is done.

Exercise for the Soft Palate

(a) Breathe in through the nose and out through the mouth, leaving the jaw wide open (a click will be heard as the soft palate moves away from the back of the tongue).

(b) Yawn with the mouth wide open and then try to yawn with the mouth closed.

(c) Repeat the words ending in NG. (DING, DONG, SING, SONG, KING, KONG, etc.)

(d) Sing M-OO-NING, M-OH-NING, M-AW-NING, M-AH-NING, M-AY-NING, M-EE-NING, gliding up and down the scale.

(A hand mirror is a most useful item whilst practising the above exercises so that the student can see how much work his organs of articulation are, in fact, doing)

Practice each of the following speech-training charts aiming for clear consonant and pure vowel sounds. Begin slowly, only quickening speed when each series can be enunciated with reasonable accuracy.

6

Open Vowels Plus Final Consonants

Oot	oht	awt	aht	ayt	eet
Ood	ohd	awd	ahd	ayd	eed
Oop	ohp	awp	ahp	ayp	eep
Oob	ohb	awb	ahb	ayb	eeb
Oof	ohf	awf	ahf	ayf	eef
Oov	ohv	awv	ahv	ayv	eev
Ook	ohk	awk	ahk	ayk	eek
Oog	ohg	awg	ahg	ayg	eeg
		("g" as in "egg")			
Oos	ohs	aws	ahs	ays	ees
Ooz	ohz	awz	ahz	ayz	eez
Oosh	ohsh	awsh	ahsh	aysh	eesh
Ooge	ohge	awge	ahge	ayge	eege
		("ge" as in "rouge")			
Ooch	ohch	awch	ahch	aych	eech
		("ch" as in "each")			
Ooj	ohj	awj	ahj	ayj	eej
		("j" as in "judge")			
Oost	ohst	awst	ahst	ayst	eest
Oosts	ohsts	awsts	ahsts	aysts	eests
Ooth	ohth	awth	ahth	ayth	eeth
Ooths	ohths	awths	ahths	ayths	eeths
Oodth	ohdth	awdth	ahdth	aydth	eedth
Oodths	ohdths	awdths	ahdths	aydths	eedths
Oom	ohm	awm	ahm	aym	eem
Ool	ohl	awl	ahl	ayl	eel

Open Vowels, Initial Consonants, Final M for Resonance

[handwritten: dropped jaw] *[handwritten: 'or']*

ɑː	ɔː	oʊ	eɪ	iː	ɑɪ	ɔɪ
BAHM	BAWM	BOHM	BAYM	BEEM	BYM	BOYM
PAHM	PAWM	POHM	PAYM	PEEM	PYM	POYM
TAHM	TAWM	TOHM	TAYM	TEEM	TYM	TOYM
DAHM	DAWM	DOHM	DAYM	DEEM	DYM	DOYM
FAHM	FAWM	FOHM	FAYM	FEEM	FYM	FOYM
VAHM	VAWM	VOHM	VAYM	VEEM	VYM	VOYM
GAHM	GAWM	GOHM	GAYM	GEEM	GYM	GOYM
KAHM	KAWM	KOHM	KAYM	KEEM	KYM	KOYM
SAHM	SAWM	SOHM	SAYM	SEEM	SYM	SOYM
ZAHM	ZAWM	ZOHM	ZAYM	ZEEM	ZYM	ZOYM
*THAHM	THAWM	THOHM	THAYM	THEEM	THYM	THOYM
†THAHM	THAWM	THOHM	THAYM	THEEM	THYM	THOYM
LAHM	LAWM	LOHM	LAYM	LEEM	LYM	LOYM
MAHM	MAWM	MOHM	MAYM	MEEM	MYM	MOYM
NAHM	NAWM	NOHM	NAYM	NEEM	NYM	NOYM
RAHM	RAWM	ROHM	RAYM	REEM	RYM	ROYM
YAHM	YAWM	YOHM	YAYM	YEEM	YYM	YOYM
WAHM	WAWM	WOHM	WAYM	WEEM	WYM	WOYM
HAHM	HAWM	HOHM	HAYM	HEEM	HYM	HOYM
WHAHM	WHAWM	WHOHM	WHAYM	WHEEM	WHYM	WHOYM
SHAHM	SHAWM	SHOHM	SHAYM	SHEEM	SHYM	SHOYM
CHAHM	CHAWM	CHOHM	CHAYM	CHEEM	CHYM	CHOYM
JAHM	JAWM	JOHM	JAYM	JEEM	JYM	JOYM

*TH as in the word THIGH.
†TH as in the word THY.

Shut Vowels with Difficult Consonant Clusters

ABTHS	EBTHS	IBTHS	OBTHS	UBTHS
ADTHS	EDTHS	IDTHS	ODTHS	UDTHS
AFTHS	EFTHS	IFTHS	OFTHS	UFTHS
AGTHS	EGTHS	IGTHS	OGTHS	UGHTS
AJTHS	EJTHS	IJTHS	OJTHS	UJTHS
AKTHS	EKTHS	IKTHS	OKTHS	UKTHS
ALTHS	ELTHS	ILTHS	OLTHS	ULTHS
AMTHS	EMTHS	IMTHS	OMTHS	UMTHS
ANTHS	ENTHS	INTHS	ONTHS	UNTHS
APTHS	EPTHS	IPTHS	OPTHS	UPTHS
ASTHS	ESTHS	ISTHS	OSTHS	USTHS
AVTHS	EVTHS	IVTHS	OVTHS	UVTHS
AXTHS	EXTHS	IXTHS	OXTHS	UXTHS
AZTHS	EZTHS	IZTHS	OZTHS	UZTHS
ABST	EBST	IBST	OBST	UBST
ABSTS	EBSTS	IBSTS	OBSTS	UBSTS
ADST	EDST	IDST	ODST	UDST
ADSTS	EDSTS	IDSTS	ODSTS	UDSTS
AFST	EFST	IFST	OFST	UFST
AFSTS	EFSTS	IFSTS	OFSTS	UFSTS
AGST	EGST	IGST	OGST	UGST
AGSTS	EGSTS	IGSTS	OGSTS	UGSTS
AKST	EKST	IKST	OKST	UKST
AKSTS	EKSTS	IKSTS	OKSTS	UKSTS
ALST	ELST	ILST	OLST	ULST
ALSTS	ELSTS	ILSTS	OLSTS	ULSTS
AMST	EMST	IMST	OMST	UMST
AMSTS	EMSTS	IMSTS	OMSTS	UMSTS
ANST	ENST	INST	ONST	UNST
ANSTS	ENSTS	INSTS	ONSTS	UNSTS
APST	EPST	IPST	OPST	UPST
APSTS	EPSTS	IPSTS	OPSTS	UPSTS
AST	EST	IST	OST	UST
ASTS	ESTS	ISTS	OSTS	USTS
AVST	EVST	IVST	OVST	UVST
AVSTS	EVSTS	IVSTS	OVSTS	UVSTS
AZSTS	EZSTS	IZSTS	OZSTS	UZSTS

9

Shut Vowels Plus Initial and Final Consonants

PAP	PEP	PIP	POP	PUP
BAB	BEB	BIB	BOB	BUB
TAT	TET	TIT	TOT	TUT
DAD	DED	DID	DOD	DUD
FAF	FEF	FIF	FOF	FUF
VAV	VEV	VIV	VOV	VUV
GAG	GEG	GIG	GOG	GUG
KAK	KEK	KIK	KOK	KUK
SAS	SES	SIS	SOS	SUS
ZAZ	ZEZ	ZIZ	ZOZ	ZUZ
*THATH	THETH	THITH	THOTH	THUTH
†THATH	THETH	THITH	THOTH	THUTH
LAL	LEL	LIL	LOL	LUL
MAM	MEM	MIM	MOM	MUM
NAN	NEN	NIN	NON	NUN
SHASH	SHESH	SHISH	SHOSH	SHUSH
CHACH	CHECH	CHICH	CHOCH	CHUCH
STAST	STEST	STIST	STOST	STUST
STASTS	STESTS	STISTS	STOSTS	STUSTS

* TH as in the word THIGH.

† TH as in the word THY

Figure of Eight Exercise

This is a particularly beneficial exercise and the rhythm of the vowel pattern helps to overcome any tension which might be felt by some students when practising the other consonant and vowel charts.

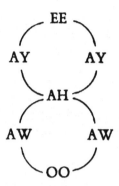

Begin by putting a consonant before each vowel, e.g. TAH TAY TEE TAY TAH TAW TOO TAW.

Then place a consonant after each vowel, e.g. AHT AYT EET AYT AHT AWT OOT AWT.

Finally, place a consonant in before and after each vowel, e.g. TAHT. TAYT TEET TAYT TAHT TAWT TOOT TAWT.

Repeat each figure of eight three times.

Use also the following consonant sounds: P.B. D. F.V. L.R. S.Z. M.N. K.G. SH. CH.

Tongue Twisters

Tongue twisters provide an amusing supplement to the fore-going speech-training charts, but their effectiveness should not be underestimated.

(*a*) Whisper the "twisters".

(*b*) Speak them with the teeth clenched (this makes the tongue and lips work more vigorously)

(*c*) Speak them with good tone and firm articulation. Slowly but clearly.

(*d*) Speak the "twisters" more and more quickly still retaining clarity of articulation.

P   Peter Piper picked a peck of pickled pepper, a peck of pickled pepper Peter Piper picked, if Peter Piper picked a peck of pickled pepper, where is the peck of pickled pepper Peter Piper picked.

B   Betty Botter bought some butter, but she said this butter's bitter. If I mix it with my batter it will make my batter bitter. So she bought some better butter and she mixed it with her batter, and she made her batter better.

T   Tommy and Tina were tattooed in Tooting, but Tommy was only tattooed on his toe, so Tommy told Tina where Tommy was tattooed, but Tina said Tommy's tattoo wouldn't show.

S–SH To sit in solemn silence in a dull dark dock, in a pestilential prison with a lifelong lock, awaiting the sensation of a short, sharp shock. From a cheap and chippy chopper, on a big black block.

P–G Five plump peas, in a peapod pressed, one grew, and two grew, and so did all the rest, grew and grew and grew and grew, and grew and never stopped, till they grew so plump and portly that the peapod popped.

B Bibby Bobby bought a bat, Bibby Bobby bought a ball, with that bat he banged the ball. Banged it bump against the wall, but so boldly Bobby banged, soon he burst the rubber ball. Boo sobbed Bobby, goodbye ball. Bad luck, Bobby, bad luck ball. Now to drown his many troubles, Bibby Bobby's blowing bubbles.

G A gregarious gaggle of geese, giggling on towards Greece, when a goose with both goggles and candour said, why don't you land in Uganda?

S Slowly and silently the stately ship, slid down the Ship's Slipway.

R-L-Y Red leather, Yellow leather, Red lorry, Yellow lorry.

K A cricket critic met with a critical crisis.

T A tutor who tooted the lute,
   Tried to tutor two tooters to toot,
   Said the two to the tutor,
   "Is it easier to toot,
   Or to tutor two tooters to toot."

R Around the rugged rock ruthless Robert ran,
   He ran around and round the rock until he met a man,
   The man was really very rude and he to Robert said,
   "Run right down to Richmond Park"—away then Robert sped.

M Many mighty men making money in the moonshine,
   Many mighty men making money in the sun,
   Many were the times they made money in the moonshine,
   Many many more did they labour in the Sun.

F-V   Fat men are funny men, thin men are not,
      Fat men are filled with joy, thin men say "rot"
      Very very few of them feel the call of spring,
      Only one or two of them ever learn to sing.

L   Lucy and Lily and laconic Bill,
      Lived all together alone on a hill,
      Lucy and Lily would only eat lamb,
      Billy liked rabbit and blackcurrant jam,
      Lucy and Lily and laconic Bill,
      Liked to lie down after eating their fill.

D   Donald the duck liked to dance a jig daily,
      Donald the duck liked to dress up to dine,
      Dutifully Donald would wear his white dicky,
      And then with the lady ducks waddle in line.

TH   Theo Thistler, the thistle sifter, sifted a sieve of sifted
      thistles into a sieve of unsifted thistles, then sifted a
      sieve of unsifted thistles into a sieve of sifted thistles,
      for Theo Thistler was a thistle sifter.

S SH   Shiela is selling her shop at the seashore,
  Z   For shops at the seashore are sure to lose,
      At her shop on the seashore should Shiela sell shell-
        fish?
      Or should she sell, sandpaper, sherry and shoes?

Ng   Sending a ring through the post was plain sailing,
      Sending a ring through the mails was just fine,
      Writing a note to his girl friend and hailing,
      A taxi, to take it to Ealing on time.

K   Kenneth the coalman's a comical cove,
      Carting his coals to Kew,
      He carries his sacks from a kiosk in Hove,
      In a sack on his back, painted blue.

M-N   Are you copper bottoming 'em my man?
No, I'm alluminuming 'em mum.

TH   The Lieth Police dismisseth us—The Lieth Police are thorough
The Lieth Police admitteth us into their lawful borough.

P-B   Peggy Babcock, Peggy Babcock, Peggy Babcock,
The Clerk to the Magistrates called
Peggy Babcock, Peggy Babcock, Peggy Babcock,
His voice down the corridor bawled
Peggy Babcock, Peggy Babcock, Peggy Babcock,
Their Worships ask that you attend.
But reply came there none from poor Peggy
For she had gone clean round the bend.

STS   There were three ghosts,
Sitting on posts,
Eating buttered toasts,
And licking their fists,
Right up to their wrists,
Weren't they beasts.

CH   Charlie is choosey when choosing his cheeses
And cheese is a challenge when Charlie arrives
But Charlie is charming and chooses a Cheddar
He chills it, and chips it, and chops in some Chives.

H   Henry Hall hops on his heels
Hopping on heels how horrid it feels
Hopping on heels isn't hopping at all
Then, why not hop properly Henry Hall.

S-Z   Moses supposes his toes's are roses
Moses supposes erroneously
Moses supposes his toes's are roses
Yes, Moses supposes his toes's to be.

15

W-Ch	If a woodchuck would chuck wood, the wood that a woodchuck would chuck is the wood that a wood chuck could chuck, if the woodchuck that could chuck wood would chuck.
Sh-TH	I shot three shy thrushes. You shoot three shy thrushes.
SN-F	I snuff shop snuff, do you snuff shop snuff?
M-N	Many an anemone sees an enemy anemone.
L-N	Nelly knits locknit knitting.
P-B	Plain bun, plum bun, bun without plum.
Qu	Quick. Whitewash wicket quite white.
BL-R	Reds rule, blue rules.
RB	Rubber Buggy bumpers.
Sl	Slim Sam shaved six slippery chins in six seconds.
CH-Sh	Stop chop shops selling chopped shop chops.
SL	Sly Sammy sat sipping Sally's soup.
S-SH	Susan Schumann shot a solitary chamois and received a short sharp salutory shock from such shameless slaughter.
S-Sh	Should such a shapeless sash such shabby stitches show?
S-TH	Six thick thistle sticks.
S-SH	Six Swiss ships swiftly shift.
M	She stood on the balcony inexplicably mimicking him hiccupping and welcoming him in.
TH-F	Three free flow pipes.
TH-S	The sixth sick sheik's sixth sheeps sick.

R	Truly rural, purely plural, truly rurally, purely plurally.
S-K	United States twin-screw steel cruisers.
W	When does the wrist watch strap shop shut?
S-N	You sniff shop snuff. I sniff shop snuff.
FR	You can have fried fresh fish, fish fried fresh, fresh fried fish, fresh fish fried, or fish fresh fried.
P-K	A knapsack strap. A knapsack strap.
D	A dozen dozen double damask dinner napkins.
B-L	A bloke's back brake block broke.
S	A shifty snake selling snake skin slippers.
B	A bootblack blacks boots with a black blacking brush.
GL	A glowing gleam glowing green.
M-B	A box of mixed biscuits in a best mixed biscuit box.
S-Sh	A soft shot silk sash shop selling shot silk sashes.
SK	A school coal scuttle, a scuttle of school coal.
F-FL	A fly flew past Flo's flat, and a fly flew past fat Flo; is the fly that flew past fat Flo the same fly that flew past fat Flo's flat.
F-Th	A fat-thighed freak fries thick fish.
R	A truly rural frugal rulers mural.
TW	A twin track tape recorder.
K-P	A proper cup of coffee in a proper coffee copper pot.
B-L	Betty Blue blows big black bubbles.
BL	Black bugs blood.

Ch-Sh Cheryl's cheap chip shop sells cheap chips.
       Chief Sheikh, Sheep section.

SH   Does this shop stock shot silk socks with spots on?

F   Freckled-faced Florence. Freckled-face Florence.

G-WH   Gig-Whip. Gig-Whip. Gig-Whip.

L-R   He is literally literary.

L-R   High Roller, Low Rowler, Lower a Roller.

H   Heather was hoping to hop to Tahiti to hack a
       hibiscus to hang on her hat. Now Heather has hun-
       dreds of hats on her hat rack. So how will a hop to
       Tahiti help that?

S-M   I miss my Swiss miss, my Swiss miss misses me.

S-Sh   If a shop that is shipshape stocks six shipshape shop-
       soiled ships, how many shipshape shop-soiled ships
       would six shipshape ship shops stock?

MAJOR-GENERAL

I am the very model of a modern major-general,
I've information vegetable, animal, and mineral.
I know the kings of England and I quote the fights historical,
From Marathon to Waterloo, in order categorical;
I'm very well acquainted too with matters mathematical,
I understand equations, both the simple and quadratical,
About binomial theorem I'm teeming with a lot o' news—
With many cheerful facts about the square of the hypoteneuse
I'm very good at integral and differential calculus;
I know the scientific names of beings animalculous;
In short, in matters vegetable, animal, and mineral,
I am the very model of a modern Major-General.

W. S. GILBERT

Vowel Practice

Although Consonant sounds can be practised fairly easily, vowel sounds present a rather more difficult obstacle to the student. Each vowel sound (and there are twenty-four of them) needs a particular tongue and lip shaping if it is to be produced properly. However, given a tutor (or in certain cases a tape recorder) the following rhymes and jingles which have been most carefully chosen will be of especial value.

Important Points

(1) The Jaw should be relaxed leaving a space of at least three-quarters of an inch between the teeth for all vowel sounds.

(2) The Tongue tip should always touch the lower teeth. The blade of the tongue will hunch or flatten to vary the size and shape of the resonating cavity and consequently the shape of the vowel.

(3) The sounds should be placed on the centre front of the hard palate, and should be carried forward on a smooth controlled column of breath.

(4) Lips play an important part in vowel formation—they should never be stretched horizontally nor closed tensely—but should further the forward placing of the voice with appropriate forward mobility.

Open Monophthongs

OO (as in Boom)
> Dougal went out shooting,
> With Rip his poodle dog,
> He shot a wild black rooster,
> As it crooned upon a log,
> He took it home to cook it,

But found to his dismay,
That Rip his little poodle,
Had let the bird away.

AW (as in Born)
Maud and Morris went to town,
Maud she bought a fawn,
Morris bought an iron sword,
And a motor horn.
Maud and Morris returned home,
To Morecambe by the sea,
Left their treasures in the hall,
For Uncle Claud to see,
Uncle Claud was overawed,
When the gifts he spied,
Fawn, and sword, and motor horn,
To the hallstand tied.

AH (as in Barn)
How far is the farthest star?
Can I get to it by car?
Past the gate and near the path,
Where the Robins take a bath,
Up to the peak of laughter hill,
To the mast where (Says a bill).
"However fast you may travel by car,
You will never get closer to it than you are."

ER (as in Burn)
Have you heard of the bird who preferred,
Nothing so much as lemon-curd?
O. Dear it really does sound absurd,
That a bird, unperturbed and quite reserved,
Could sit in its nest eating lemon-curd.

EE (as in Bean)

> The teacher tried to teach the class,
> To eat their peas with ease,
> Mary dropped hers on the floor, Ena on the freeze,
> Said teacher to his heedless class,
> I really can't believe,
> How G.C.E. you hope to pass,
> With gravy on your sleeve.

Shut Monophthongs

OO (as in Book)

> The wooden bull hung on the hook,
> The cushion on the chair,
> The pussy on the table sat,
> Whilst the butcher combed his hair.
> His wife is always pushing him
> Around. With her full figure,
> She always wears a worsted skirt,
> Though it makes her look much bigger.

U (as in But)

> If ducks eat grain,
> And Gulls drink rain,
> And Tom eats bubble and squeak,
> If Dutchmen grow fresh poppy bulbs,
> And Welshmen grow the leek,
> If folk in London wear top hats,
> And shoes with buckles don,
> Then why have cats in England tails,
> Whilst Manx cats have got none.

O (as in Box)

> I don't like snobs who stand and scoff,
> At folk with far less money,
> Nor Dons who nod at other Dons,
> They seem to me plain funny,
> The folk I like have got warm hearts,
> And offer generosity,
> Whilst snobs and Dons are most inclined,
> To suffer from Pomposity.

A (as in Bat)

> Tap tap tap go Tina's toes,
> Tap tap tap her heels,
> Tina dances brightly,
> Scottish Strathspey reels,
> The lass has got it badly.
> Dancing all day long,
> I wish she'd marry Andy,
> Or learn to sing a song.

E (as in Bed)

> The egg rolled down the endless bank,
> The egg that Edgar rolled,
> It came to rest against a hedge,
> The egg that Edgar rolled.
> And though it may appear incredible,
> That egg was then proclaimed inedible,
> The egg that rolled right down the bank,
> The egg that Edgar rolled.

i (as in Bit)

> Tiny Tim the tinker's son,
> Tips the scales at ten stone one,
> Tiny Tim just hates to think,
> Of food to eat, and drinks to drink,

Whilst he poor boy just lives on hips,
Apple pips and boiled cow-slips,
Nibbling thistle seeds all day,
Excess weight just melts away.

Diphthongs (double-sounding vowels)

OH (as in Bowl. O as in Box plus o͞o as in Book)
    In our town there lives a Yeoman,
    Whose as old, as old can be,
    He claims to be an ancient Roman,
    And he always smiles at me.
    Although I know he is a Yeoman,
    And in Oldham makes his home,
    I can't believe he is a Roman,
    Who saw the glory that was Rome.

OW (as in Bound. U as in But plus o͞o as in Bush)
    One night there howled a loud-mouthed owl,
    A mouse was roused out from its bed,
    And frowned round at the shouting owl,
    Who's loud-mouthed shout made him see red.
    He howled "To town is where I'm bound,
    From plough and fowl to house and crowd,"
    He howled away into the night,
    That noisy owl filled with delight.

OI (as in Boy. Aw as in Saw plus i as in Bit)
    A little boy who's name was Roy,
    For his birthday got a toy,
    He was so pleased until he tried,
    To see the springs and works inside.
    Alas the engine broke in two,
    And the boy he cried "Boo Hoo",
    Father came and fixed the toy,
    Oil on waters renewed joy.

I (as in Bite . **U** as in But plus **i** as in Hit)
> I spied Ida eating Ivor's Ice cream,
> I spied Ida licking Ivor's Ice,
> I cried, "Ida, it really isn't nice cream,
> Ivor bought it yesterday to poison all the mice".

AY (as in Blake. **E** as in Bet plus **i** as in Bit)
> David Yates has gained in weight,
> From eight stone five to eight stone eight.
> He walks quite slowly through the gate,
> To contemplate his excess weight.
> He eats no cakes, neglects his tea,
> For he has every faith,
> That dieting will turn the scales,
> From eight stone eight to eight stone three.

EW (as in Beauty. **I** as in Bit plus **oo** as in Book)
> A Mule who's name was Hugh,
> Liked eating Irish stew,
> He refused to eat raw carrots,
> And turnips from a bag,
> He only would pay tribute,
> This puking, fuming nag,
> When stew was on the menu,
> His rear end he would wag.

AIR (as in Bear. **E** as in Bear plus **ə** as in The)
> It isn't fair said the big black bear,
> For carefree folk to come and stare,
> When I dance at the County fair,
> People come from here and there,
> To see the fairy-footed bear.

EER (as in Fear. **I** as in Bit plus **ə** as in The)
> Old King Lear was rather queer,
> His beard was white, his eyes so clear,

Three daughters had he, and 'twas true,
His life was in a dreadful stew,
He ate much food and drank much beer,
And so he lived from year to year.

OOR (as in Boorish. Oo as in Book plus ə as in The)
The old man on the moor,
Who lived there all alone,
Was really very poor,
You never heard him moan,
He sang all day, and danced all night,
And filled the tourists with delight.

Triphtongs (diphthongs plus the neutral vowel as in THE)

OUR (as in Bower. U plus oo plus ə)
In a bower,
Near a tower,
Lived a Scotsman,
Called Glendower,
Big he was,
And full of power,
And his one joy,
Was a flower.

IRE (as in Fire. U plus i plus ə)
Never Tire of Choirboys,
Never Tire of Lyres,
Don't forget to iron out,
Trouble with the Squires,
A liar never call your friend,
Nor set your house on fire,
If you would reach your journey's end,
And meet your heart's desire.

URE (as in Cure. I plus ŏo plus ə)
> The water in the sewer,
> Can never be thought pure,
> For me it has no lure,
> So few and even fewer,
> Of the doctors find a cure,
> For the water in the sewer.

———————————

ER	er*	a	e	i	EE
lurk	Ascot	lack	neck	flick	meek
worth	mathematics	hath	death	pith	heath
worship	linen	man	never	live	league
earl	bargain	flag	egg	fig	meal
herb	collect	shall	gem	still	seen
firm	cannot	vat	tell	tin	beat
learn	accord	mad	deaf	dish	leash
furze	problem	sham	heather	whiffle	fleeting
pert	sauce-pan	gaff	Keppel	fitting	plead
worthy	children	dabble	fetch	limb	seizure
surf	about	map	rep	nip	beam
herd	of(t)en	azure	pleasure	stiff	leap
nerve	irrevocable	have	fen	fit	feeble
furry	centenary	marry	wherry	lyric	he
learns	barracks	fans	hens	spins	leans
burden	vegetables	dazzles	cells	widths	heaths
nurse	tortoise	lass	mess	hiss	beef
merge	suppose	dad	ebb	nib	heave
lurch	admonish	lash	betting	fissure	peace
earning	China	spanning	vessel	wriggle	eagle
world	lilacs	dandled	pelt	built	yield
Myrtle	continually	prattle	metal	little	secretion
gurgle	consist	stand	edible	nibble	people
nursling	acknowledge	has	net	rid	breathe
purple	adhesion	badge	edge	midge	teach
earths	phonetics	asp	Esk	risk	least
burble	vegetable	hatch	heckle	tickle	teazle
earned	condition	apple	mend	ditch	breeze
first	private	snaffle	rest	pinned	weaned
irksome	agenda	stab	led	with	treacle
early	penance	tassel	mesh	is	leeks
furls	material	tackle	Nelly	nipple	mealy
berthed	India	valley	sevenths	mist	heat
turfs	ornament	bat	bet	bidden	beetle
girl	mountain	hammer	deaden	miller	peals
version	listen	madden	chef's	tiffs	wreathed
curves	system	gaffs	cellar	mission	briefs
bird	captain	fashion	guess	gives	sleeves
pearl	problem	hast	hen	mills	dealer
burn	suggestion	waggle	said	thistle	bee

* The neutral vowel as in "the".

27

OO	oo	AW	o	AH	u
through	hook	stalk	flock	mark	duck
stool	bull	morgue	flog	target	mug
lose	brook	cause	was	pass	fuss
booby	shook	warp	stop	harp	up
boon	foot	maul	doll	darn	gull
moot	good	fawn	gone	dart	fun
prove	pull	wharf	of	starve	love
toothing	butcher	awning	stopping	darning	cunning
tool	wolf	morsel	jostle	parcel	hustle
soup	woman	coursed	bosky	mast	dust
cooled	pulled	mauled	lolled	hearths	cult
spoons	cushion	portion	dons	glance	percussion
ooze	bullet	bought	offer	raft	but
troop	bushes	George	Tommy	grass	mumps
rule	crooked	northern	trodden	transport	London
mood	cook	sought	lot	arm	but
rouge	hood	porch	topple	harsh	mother
wound	rook	dawned	wand	sparkle	supple
tooth	stood	orb	Tom	laugh	mud
loom	puss	forth	odd	bath	some
soup	push	ford	mob	father	rub
roof	book	course	notch	dance	stuff
Dougal	should	bauble	hobble	aunt	budge
booths	fully	Norsk	dodge	hasp	buzz
quadruple	worsted	forge	moth	sample	hush
smoothed	wood	hoary	floss	marble	Dutch
soothe	pushing	fourths	off	path	bubble
spook	bulls	form	bosh	castle	muffle
loose	cuckoo	halls	joggle	branch	fund
Scrooge	put	wharf's	lost	startle	buckle
roost	shook	pawns	sorry	pardon	dully
pools	pulpet	mortal	dolls	ask	buns
roofs	sugar	warden	Goths	Derby	mumps
poodle	wooden	soar	toddle	grant	come
boon	could	ball	box	glass	flutter
hooves	woollen	sport	strong	draught	scuttle
cool	took	tall	block	prance	muffs
food	fuller	wharves	folly	France	loves
cooler	pudding	fall	doffs	plant	smuggle
moon	bullion	warm	fodder	slant	hurry

28

OOR	AIR	EAR	URE	OUR	IRE
poor	heiress	heir	immure	cower	fiery
sure	shear	pier	pure	coward	lion
touring	pear	weary	curable	Devoner	hire
contour	wares	ears	pursuer	power	buyer
amour	affair	pierce	aperture	sour	fired
brochure	aware	fear	ewers	hour	iron
pporly	cairn	beer	jury	towel	friar
jury	hair	weir	endureth	hourly	bias
bournes	bairn	sear	steward	flowering	pliers
paramour	fairly	bier	secure	flowery	liar
moor	fairy	area	purer	shower	wire
moored	beware	cheer	during	showery	ironed
boor	air	leer	purely	bowel	dire
tours	bear	shear	fury	dowered	fire
doer	bairns	tear	lured	flowereth	iodine
truer	dare	gear	liqueur	bowers	prior
wooer	stared	reared	viewer	dowager	Isaiah
poorer	careth	neareth	adjure	plougher	tireth
adjure	share	here	curing	tower	byre
boorish	careless	nearing	endure	Maori	lyres
Ruhr	mayor	fierce	sewer	trowel	tiring
brewer	various	nearly	newer	vowel	spire
spoor	rare	eerie	cure	allowance	choir
gourd	pairing	appear	lurid	flour	diary
plural	fairer	fear	epicure	scour	sire
rural	stair	beard	Muriel	devower	friar
juror	e'er	theatre	miniature	disavowel	pyre
tournament	prayer	aria	spurious	rowel	Messiah

OH	OW	OY	I	AY	EW
oafs	mouthed	hoist	reprisal	eighths	duly
cloves	owls	loins	trifle	mailed	dukes
yokel	howled	coined	bible	flails	used
ocean	crowding	foist	mines	hazel	tube
rose	gouge	rejoyce	hives	mate	dupe
close	couch	soil	fifes	able	fume
tone	account	noise	finer	lathe	fugure
mole	ground	joint	bite	faith	puke
rogue	sound	Roy	title	lave	few
stove	town	loiter	life	pain	cute
loaf	tousle	joyeth	gibe	mail	lieu
robe	about	voice	type	vague	ewer
moan	noun	boys	lies	make	huge
coal	fowl	join	ice	reign	feudal
total	brow	avoid	lithe	paler	mule
motion	gown	soiled	wily	maiden	fuchsia
loans	cowry	boiler	pikes	laves	fuse
coach	allow	hoyden	bind	waifs	puce
closure	joust	boils	vile	bathed	nude
ode	down	toiled	buy	aiming	duty
note	shout	foil	like	stage	tune
oak	loud	voyage	child	H. (aitch)	lute
alone	clown	purloin	sigh	shape	stewed
hope	clout	oyster	pie	fame	suit
soul	cloud	coif	high	fade	feud
holes	found	loin	kind	late	usury
moult	drown	foil	bite	waste	huge
clothes	round	coin	shine	gained	puling
most	prouder	boy	tide	babe	bugle
owned	growl	point	lime	safe	duet
home	cow	void	dive	mace	pure
mope	mouth	toiling	python	maze	puled
only	mouse	yoicks	piling	bay	dunes
noble	rouse	oily	try	maple	fusion
pole	frowns	poise	aisle	save	mute
loathe	pound	poison	why	aches	abuse
oath	bound	loyal	mind	daily	beauty
roaming	hound	toy	dye	trains	assume
oaks	mound	royal	miles	nation	cue
wholly	brown	adroit	scythed	fatal	muse

MODULATION

Modulation means the musical and variable qualities of the speaking voice, which include Pitch, Pace, Inflection, Volume and Intensity, with the use of pausing. A well modulated voice will always score over a monotonous one and the speaker who varies his delivery must stand a much greater chance of getting a sympathetic hearing. Of course, the mood and style of what is being said, will serve to indicate how it should be correctly modulated.

A harsh voice will gain much from the speaking of lyrical poetry and an over-musical voice should be much improved after its owner has been restricted to strong dramatic narrative for a period.

The student should read aloud from as many varied plays, poems and prose as he can lay his hands on, and through his imagination and technique he should endeavour to bring the cold print to life.

As you perform the following exercise try to give each of the descriptions its full sound values.

Soft snow falling, drifting. Brittle ice crackling, cracking. Bumble bees humming, murmuring. Sad voices wailing, moaning. Rain spots dripping, dropping. Small bells tinkling, jingling. Solemn bells tolling, knolling. Gay bells chiming, ringing. Wild winds whistling, shrilling. Huge crags rocking, crashing. Sheets of rain lashing, splashing. Distant drums throbbing, tapping. Threatening thunder rolling, rumbling. Strong oars straining, creaking. Brilliant diamonds glimmering, glittering. Faint echoes fading, dying. Hot sunshine glowing, burning. Clear moonlight shining, beaming. Noisy trains shrieking, rushing. Swift lightning flashing, fleeting. Strange dreams hovering, haunting. Sharp frost nipping, biting. Lazy water lapping, slapping. Crisp rivulets running, rippling. Harsh saws rasping, tearing. Pale ghosts wandering, drifting. Light feet tripping, skipping. Bright stars twinkling, sparkling. Small birds twittering, tweeting. Fierce trumpets braying, shrilling. Bright flags flying, fluttering. Dry leaves whispering, rustling. Busy brooks prattling, babbling. Wet soap slipping, sliding. Tongues of fire leaping, flaming. Night skies darkening, deepening.

Finally: Your voice must be your own—don't try to imitate someone else's. You don't need to. Your main task should be to discover it and to set about developing its vast potentialities. This must prove to be a rich and most rewarding experience to all who seek for truth and beauty in life.

Students of Speech training are urged never to use good poetry or prose for articulation or vowel practice. This can only result in destroying the beauty of the pieces for ever and is to be deplored.

When poetry or prose is spoken aloud then the attention should be focused on the expression and interpretation of the material.

Simple rhymes and jingles, such as the ones which I have included in the foregoing sections are all that need be used for practice. The student should attempt to invent some more for himself.

PRONUNCIATION

"The flowering moments of the mind drop half their petals in our speech."

RALPH WALDO EMERSON, 1803-82

There is in Great Britain, though this is by no means universal, a particular type of pronunciation which is known as Standard English. This is defined as the type of Speech used by Educated or Cultured people and because it is classless and untainted by regional differences it is often regarded as being more acceptable than is a regional accent. It is also constantly changing, like fashion in dress. The purpose of speech is to communicate our thoughts to other people with the least possible difficulty on both sides, so it follows that the use of Standard English will enable us to do this more effectively and efficiently.

This does not mean that individuality in the speaker will be lost. Personality is revealed through tone, tempo, pitch, rhythm and modulation, which no-one could standardize even if they wanted to. Faults in pronunciation can usually be traced to incorrect vowel sounds—remember Eliza Doolittle trying to change "The Rine in Spine" into the more acceptable "Rain in Spain"? So the student should make a special effort first to listen to good speech (the B.B.C. news readers set a very high standard and there are dozens of excellent L.P. Spoken English records available on the market), then he can try to replace the faulty sounds in his own speech with pure ones. If he really desires to acquire the Standard pronunciation of English providing that he has a good ear and is prepared to work at it, the student should not find the transformation too difficult.

33

I am including a list of words containing every vowel sound in the English language which will be of practical use to anyone who is keen to bring about this transformation. I am also including an amusing poem which points out the many difficulties and pitfalls of pronunciation. After he has read it, the student may decide to buy a good dictionary. This is my reason for including "The Chaos".

THE CHAOS

Dearest creature in Creation,
Studying English pronunciation,
   I will teach you in my verse
   Sounds like corpse, corps, horse and worse,
It will keep you, Susy, busy,
Make your head with heat grow dizzy,
   Tear in eye your dress you'll tear,
   Queer, fair seer, hear my prayer,
Pray, console your loving poet,
Make my coat look new, dear, sew it!
   Just compare heart, beard and heard,
   Pies and diet, lord and word,
Sword and guard, retain and Britain,
(Mind the latter, how it's written)
   Made has not the sound of bade;
   Say, said, pay, paid, laid and plaid.
Now I surely will not plague you
With such words as vague and ague,
   But be careful how you speak,
   Say gush, bush, steak, streak, break, bleak,
Woven, oven, how and low,
   Script, receipt, shoe, poem, toe,
Hear me say, devoid of trickery;
Daughter, laughter and Terpsichore,

Typhoid, measles, topsails, aisles,
Exciles, similes, reviles,
Wholly, holly, signal, signing,
Same, examining, but mining,
  Scholar, vicar and cigar,
  Solar, mica, war and far.
From "desire": desirable—admirable from "admire";
Lumber, plumber, bier and brier,
  Topsham, brougham, renown but known,
  Knowledge, drone, lone, gone, none, tone,
One, anemone, Balmoral,
Kitchen, lichen, laundry, laurel,
  Gertrude, German, wind and wind;
  Scene, Melpomene, mankind,
Tortoise, turquoise, chamois-leather,
Reading, Reading, heathen, heather,
  This phonetic labyrinth,
  Gives moss, gross, brook, brooch, ninth, plinth.
Billet does not end like ballet,
Bouquet, wallet, mallet, chalet.
  Blood and flood are not like food,
  Nor is mould like should and would.
Banquet is not nearly parquet,
Which exactly rhymes with khaki.
  Discount, viscount, load and broad,
  Toward, to forward, no reward.
Ricocheted and croqueting, croquet?
Right! Your pronunciation's O.K.;
  Rounded, wounded, grieve and sieve,
  Friend and fiend, alive and live.
  Hugh but hug and hood but hoot,
  Buoyant, minute but minute.
Twopence, threepence, tease are easy,
But cease, greasy, grease and greasy?
Venice, nice, valise, revise,

Rabies but lullabies.
Would you like some more? You'll have it;
David, affidavit, davit,
Calico, but caliph. Sheik
Has the sound of Czech or ache.
Liberty, library, heave and heaven,
Rachel, eache, moustache, eleven
We say hallowed but allowed,
People, leopard, towed but vowed.
Mark the difference moreover,
Between mover, plover, Dover,
Leeches, breeches, wise, precise,
Chalice but police and lice,
Camel, constable, unstable,
Principle, disciple, label,
Petal, penal and canal,
Wait, surmise, plait, promise, pal,
But it is not hard to tell,
Why it's pall, mall but Pall Mall.
Muscle, muscular, goal iron,
Timber, climber, bullion, lion,
Worm and storm, chaise, chaos, chair,
Senator, spectator, mayor.
Ivy, Privy, famous. Clamour
Has the a of drachm and "hammer",
Pussy, hussy and possess,
Desert but desert, address,
Golf, wolf, countenance; lieutenants
Hoist, in lieu of flags, left pennants.
Courier, courtier, tomb, bomb, comb,
Cow but Cowper, some and home.
Stranger does not rhyme with anger,
Neither does devour with clangour.
Soul but foul and gaunt but aunt;
Font, front, wont, want, grand and, grant,

Arsenic, specific, scenic,
Relic, rhetoric, hygienic,
Gooseberry, goose, and close but close,
Paradise, rise, rose, and dose.
Say inveigh, neigh but inveigle,
Make the latter rhyme with eagle,
Mind! Meandering but mean,
Serpentine, and magazine.
And I bet you, dear, a penny,
You say mani(fold) like many,
Which is wrong. Say rapier, pier,
Tier (one who ties) but tier.
Arch archangel! Pray, does erring
Rhyme with herring, or with stirring?
Prison, bison, treasure-trove,
Treason, hover, cover, cove.
Perseverance, severance. Ribald
Rhymes (but piebald doesn't) with nibbled
Phaeton, paean, gnat, ghat, gnaw,
Lien phthisic, shone, bone, pshaw.
Don't be down, my own, but rough it,
And distinguish buffet—buffet;
Brood, stood, roof, rook, school, wool, stool,
Worcester, Boleyn, foul and ghoul.
Now you need not pay attention
To such sounds as I don't mention,
Sounds like pores, pause, pours, and paws,
Rhyming with the pronoun yours;
Nor are proper names included,
Though I often heard, as you did,
Funny rhymes to unicorn,
Yes, you know them: Vaughan and Strachan.
No, my maiden, fair and comely,
I don't want to speak of Cholmondeley,
No. Yet Froude, compared with proud,

Is no better than Mcleod.
But mind trivial and vial,
Tripod, menial, denial,
Troll and trolley, realm and ream,
Schedule, mischief, schism and scheme.
Had this invalid invalid
Worthless documents? How pallid,
How uncouth he, couchant, looked,
When for Portsmouth I had booked!
Zeus, Thebes, Thales, Aphrodite,
Paramour, enamoured, flighty!
Episodes, antipodes,
Acquiesce, and obsequies.
Pious, impious, limb, climb, comely,
Worsted, worsted, crumbly, dumbly,
Conquer, conquest, breathed, breathed, fan,
Wan, Sedan and artisan.
The "th" will surely trouble you
More than "r", "ch" or "w",
May then these phonetic gems:
Thomas, thyme, Theresa, Thames,
Thomson, Chatham, Waltham, Streatham,
There are more, but I forget 'em—
Wait! I've got it: Anthony,
Lighten your anxiety.
Shoes, goes, does.* Now first say: finger;

* No, you are wrong. This is the plural of doe.

Then say: singer, ginger, linger.
Real, zeal, mauve, gauze and gauge,
Marriage, foliage, mirage, age.
Hero, heron, query, very,
Parry, tarry, fury, bury,
Dost, lost, post and doth, cloth, loth,
Job, Job, blossom, bosom, oath.

Seat, sweat, chase, caste, Leigh, eight, height,
Put, nut, granite and unite.
Reefer does not rhyme with deafer,
Feoffer does, and zephyr, heifer,
Dull, bull, Geoffrey, George, ate late,
Hint, pint, senate but sedate,
Gaelic, Arabic, pacific,
Science, conscience, scientific,
Tour but our and succour, four,
Gas, alas and Arkansas.
Sea, idea, guinea, area,
Psalm, Maria but malaria,
Youth, south, southern, cleanse and clean,
Doctrine, turpentine, marine,
Compare alien with Italian,
Dandelion with battalion,
Rally with ally; yea, ye,
Eye, I, ay, aye, whey, key, quay.
Say aver, but ever, fever,
Neither, leisure, skein, receiver,
Never guess—it is not safe:
We say calves, valves, half, but Ralph.
Starry, granary, canary,
Crevice but device and eyrie,
Face but preface, but grimace,
Phlegm, plegmatic, ass, glass, bass,
Bass, large, target, gin give, verging,
Ought, oust, joust and scour but scourging,
Ear but earn, and wear and tear
Do not rhyme with "here", but "ere",
Pudding, puddle, putting. Putting?
Yes. At golf it rhymes with "shutting".
Respite, spite, consent resent,
Liable but Parliament.
Seven is right, but so is even,

Hyphen, roughen, nephew, Stephen
Monkey, donkey, clerk and jerk,
Asp, grasp, wasp, demesne, cork, work.
"A" of valour, vapid, vapour,
"S" of news (compare newspaper),
"G" of gibbet, gibbon, gist,
"I" of antichrist and grist
Differ, like diverse and divers,
Rivers, strivers, shivers, fivers,
Once but nonce, toll, doll but roll,
Polish, Polish, poll and poll.
Pronunciation—think of psyche!—
Is a paling, stout and spikey;
It's a dark abyss or tunnel,
Strewn with stones, like rowlock, gunwale;
Islington and Isle of Wight,
Housewife, verdict and indict.
Don't you think so, reader, rather,
Saying lather, bather, father?
Finally: which rhymes with "enough",
Though, through, plough, cough, hough, or touch?
Hiccough has the sound of "sup" . . .
My advise is—give it up!

ANONYMOUS

APPENDIX

I have chosen twelve speeches from Shakespeare, each one requiring a different mood or emotion. Study the complete play first and then *act* the scene, imagining that you are wearing the appropriate costume. This is one of the most enjoyable ways of developing vocal range, projection and sincere modulation of voice and speech.

Impatience   *Romeo and Juliet*   Act II, Scene 5
from   "The clock struck nine when I did send the nurse . . .
to   . . . Hast thou met with him? Send thy man away."

Revenge   *Julius Caesar*   Act III, Scene 1
from   "O, pardon me, thou bleeding piece of earth . . .
to   . . . With carrion men, groaning for burial."

Inspiration   *As You Like It*   Act I, Scene 3
from   "I did not then entreat to have her stay . . .
to   . . . Say what thou canst, I'll go along with thee."
          (Speak only Celia's part, omitting Duke Frederick's and Rosalind's lines)

Horror   *Macbeth*   Act II, Scene 1
from   "Is this a dagger which I see before me . . .
to   . . . That summons thee to heaven or to hell."

Dejection   *King Henry IV, Part II*   Act III, Scene 1
from   "How many thousand of my poorest subjects . . .
to   . . . Uneasy lies the head that wears a crown."

Doubt   *Hamlet*   Act III, Scene 1
from   "To be, or not to be—that is the question . . .
to   . . . And lose the name of action."

Impish Fun   *A Midsummer Night's Dream* Act III, Scene 2
from   "My mistress with a monster is in love . . .
to   . . . Titania waked, and straightway loved an ass."

Triumph   *King Henry V*   Act IV, Scene 3
from   "This day is call'd the feast of Crispian . . .
to   . . . That fought with us upon Saint Crispin's day."

Humour   *The Merchant of Venice*   Act I, Scene 1
from   "Let me play the fool . . .
to   . . . I'll end my exhortation after dinner."

Deliberation   *The Merchant of Venice*   Act II, Scene 2
from   "Certainly my conscience will serve me to run . . .
to   . . . my heels are at your command; I will run."

Plea for Mercy   *The Merchant of Venice*   Act IV, Scene 1
from   "The quality of mercy is not strain'd . . .
to   . . . Must needs give sentence 'gainst the merchant
          there."

Tranquillity   *The Merchant of Venice*   Act V, Scene 1
from   "How sweet the moonlight sleeps upon this bank . . .
to   . . . Doth grossly close it in, we cannot hear it."

Made with the following organs of speech

Nature of Sound	Lips	Tongue-tip and hard palate	Back of tongue and soft palate	Tongue-tip and top teeth	Tongue and hard palate	Tongue and hard palate and lips	Top teeth and bottom lip	Open mouth and throat	Semi-vowels	
									Lip-rounding	Hard palate and body of tongue
EXPLOSIVE — BREATH (unvoced)	P p	T t	K k		CH (choke) tʃ					
EXPLOSIVE — VOICE	B b	D d	G g		J (joke) dʒ					
CONTINUANT — BREATH (unvoced)				TH (thatch) θ	S s	SH ʃ	F f	H h	HW ʍ	
CONTINUANT — VOICE				TH (that) ð	Z z	ZH (azure) ʒ	V v		W w	Y j
Nasal sounds — L R (l r)	M m	N n	NG (sing) ŋ							

The Phonetic Symbols are given below each consonant.

43

Lightning Source UK Ltd.
Milton Keynes UK
UKOW06f1915190917
309503UK00007B/605/P